DIRT

Studies in Austrian Literature, Culture, and Thought

Translation Series

Robert Schneider

DIRT

Translated and with an Afterword by

Paul F. Dvorak

ARIADNE PRESS
Riverside, California

Ariadne Press would like to express its appreciation to the Austrian Cultural Institute, New York and the Bundesministerium für Wissenschaft, Forschung und Kunst, Vienna for assistance in publishing this book.

Translated from the German *Dreck*
©1993 Reclam Verlag Leipzig

Library of Congress Cataloging-in-Publication Data

Schneider, Robert, 1961-
    [Dreck, English]
    Dirt / Robert Schneider : translated by Paul F. Dvorak.
        p.   cm. -- (Studies in Austrian literature, culture, and thought. Translation series)
    ISBN 1-57241-023-X
    I. Dvorak, Paul F. . II. Title. III. Series.
PT2680.N376D7413   1996
832'.914--dc20

                                95-34960
                                CIP

Cover design:
Art Director: George McGinnis
Illustrator, Designer: Lora A. Kueneman

Robert Schneider

Dirt

I.

A man sells roses in the lobby.
Four marks apiece.

II.

Darkness
A man begins to speak.

My name is Sad. I'm thirty years old. In English Sad means sad. I'm not sad. Sad, Sad what? But by that point I'm running off already. A family name is one word too many. My friend, the tall Egyptian—Egyptians are also dirty—gave his family name simply because he was afraid. Now they know that he's from Port Said. Of course I have a family name, although I really don't deserve to have one. A nice-sounding family name. At least to my ears. When I shout out my family name, down below, where the subway rushes by—I push my face up against the gate by the exit—like this—when I hear the train rumbling from far off, and when the rush of air comes through that it pushes along ahead of it, and tousles my hair, and when the beam of light shines at me and blinds me, and when the noise is the loudest, I shout it out. Even though I don't have any right to shout. I know that. But sometimes a person is happy, and he doesn't want to suppress his feelings. That's when I go down to the subway. And when the beam of light shines at me, I have to shout.

He shouts.
He lights several candles.
The room gradually becomes brighter.
A frayed upholstered chair.
A plastic bucket with fifty roses.

I'm thirty years old. I dream a lot. I dream my family name. Out loud, Nabil says. The night on the roof, the flapping of the palm branches, my father, backgammon, and the tea. A lot of tea. A lot. Dreaming means not having a clear conscience. Basra. The swamps. Teheran. Ankara. Warsaw. Stockholm. And now here. I dream because I have a guilty conscience. January, the winter, the fifty-eight stops, the forty-year-old men, and eight miles every night. Sad,

Sad what? But by that point I'm running off again. I have no right to use the word dreaming. It belongs to your cats and children. I understand that. And I accept it too. Really.

He sits down.

I'm thirty years old. I'd like to say I was younger. Sometimes. When we engage in conversation. I like to talk. I tell stories. I lie. It's an innate thing with me. I have to talk. It passes the time at night. And the eight miles get shorter and the forty-year-old men smaller. I'm twenty-five. Whether I'm thirty, twenty-five, or forty, I can say one thing right away: I have no right to live here. Even though I basically love life. If a person is allowed to express it that way.
I like being in this beautiful city with the store windows that always smell of ammonia. I've never touched a store window with my fingers. Only smelled them. I swear it. I've really never done that. With my fingers, I mean. I know who I am. That comes right from the soul. The

10

filth. And that's the truth. Mm. Ammonia. Ammonia and January. Mm!

He reaches into his pocket.

This is my mother. Her hands are still warm in the picture. My uncle took the picture. With a Leica. Where I come from we only take pictures on special occasions. Her hands are still warm. I remember. That was 1980. In August. With a Leica. The word. This beautiful word! That's when it began. The longing for the German language. Only this word. Leica. That's me here. With a bald spot. Behind me, that's an old Ford. It belonged to my English teacher. She died of homesickness. The heat, the dusty streets, the noise, and the stench of fish. There's a large harbor in Basra. Incredibly dirty. She told us about Dover. There are cliffs there that are whiter than snow. Stupid me had his eyes closed in the picture. I'm not accustomed to having my picture taken. It was at the time I went off to the university. I'm a student. Philosophy has always interested me. And

German literature.

And that is Her. But we don't write each other any more. I just stopped opening her letters. It's safer. In the beginning it was like January and ammonia. Now it's okay. Really, things are going very well. It's safer.

No, I stopped opening her letters.

Actually not. I simply didn't accept them. The letters. Very simple. No mailbox, no nameplate on the door, no doorbell, heard nothing, wasn't there, didn't know anything. Didn't want to attract attention.

He speaks loudly.

Are they stupid? The guys from the secret service?! I'm a deserter! I wanted to learn German, not war!

He speaks calmly.

I start with the premise that the war was important. Even necessary. The great cities of America. The beautiful people with the pale skin. The culture and democracy. What can we do in the face of that? In pre-colonial conditions. That just has to be said. Cities without hygiene, without any infrastructure, and with a lot of desert, and practically no democracy. And backwards with regard to moral values. I say that because it's the truth. Sociologists and economists have proven it often enough. I see that myself. When one compares the pictures of the great American cities with the pictures of our cities. The pictures of the beautiful people with the pale skin. Then the war has meaning. That's the premise I start with.

She has a child. Unfortunately my uncle is already dead, and therefore there's no picture of the child. Who knows who the Leica belongs to now. He's a happy child. For sure. I wanted to give him a German name. My brother is taking care of Nihart now. He's a happy child. I believe that a person who finds himself at a primitive stage of development can live on in a person who also finds himself at a primitive stage of development. A simple thought formulated somewhat pedantically. What I want to say...Nihart is a happy child. I studied philosophy for three semesters. I know that I continue to live in Nihart. But that's not relevant here.

He is silent.

Here I am now, although I have no right to be here. In a strictly legal sense. The official agency governing foreigners.
What I especially like about this city are the park benches. There are a lot of park benches in this city. More park benches than in Basra. Pretty park benches with flourishing cast iron feet. I like to watch the people as they sit down on the bench or as they get up and leave. I just watch them. Mostly on Sunday afternoons. Although I have no right to a Sunday. I'm here illegally. The people on the benches have the right to a Sunday. I've known that since I started learning about the history of this country.
History and philosophy. I never wanted to choose. And German literature.
What I wanted to say: When the park-bench

14

people—if I may express it that way—were young, they rebuilt this city with their own hands. At that time there was a great war. Not to be compared with our war. The park-bench people were drawn in innocently. Lost their sons and families. You can't compare that with our war. First, because we stand behind our president—one merely has to look at the news agency pictures with the jubilant people—and second, because it's of no great consequence if an Arab mother loses her son. That's the truth. First of all there are lots of Arabs, and there are constantly more and more, and second of all an Arab mother can't really mourn. That's a sociological phenomenon related to the more primitive level of development. Third of all, and this also needs to be said, there's a big difference between a boy with pale skin being shot and one with dark skin. Because of the culture and the democratic system. That has to be said, and if that's too profound a thought for anybody, he should just pack up and leave.

He leaves.
He comes back with an onion.

I'm not a cynical person. A person is
cynical when he is afraid of life. If a person
may express it that way.
I could submit a petition for asylum,
although I don't have the right to do so. I'm
an Arab. Not a Kurd. Arab. Semite. I could
submit a petition. But it wouldn't go
through. I wouldn't be shot, if I were to
return. And it's a fact that only those who
would be shot have a right to asylum.
That's perfectly obvious. Because of
political persecution! It's a blanket concept.
It wouldn't help me get by. A person has to
prove that he would be shot, or at least
persecuted. Everything has its order. I could
submit a petition. But then they'd say Sad,
Sad what? You surely have a family name.
Every civilized person has a family name.
Then I already see the dark of night, and I
run away.

He bites into the onion.

By the way, what I still wanted to say about the park benches with the cast iron feet: I've never sat down on a park bench in this city. Nabil can vouch for that. My best friend. By Allah! Really never. I'd never go that far.

Okay, I occasionally use a public toilet and even have to admit that I am very particular about the cleanliness of the toilets. I know that I am gradually bringing your sewer system to the point of overflowing with my urine.

Am I the only foreigner in this city, huh?

The massive sewer systems that the park-bench people constructed in their day, when they were young. I should excrete my shit in the latrine in Basra. I would do that if I were there. In Basra. But I'm not in Basra.

The man with the windbreaker was right when he caught me as I was pulling the sleeve of my sweater over my hand to push down the door handle. The man with the windbreaker goes through life with his eyes open.

A study shows that our urine is more pungent and smells more acrid than the urine elsewhere. That's been proven. Medically. In the laboratory. There are many reasons for it. One convincing reason is that we eat raw onions by the pound. That's why our urine smells so acrid. That's a convincing reason.

The foreigner devours onions and garlic. And because he doesn't brush his teeth, he has bad breath. I've never contested that. Have I? Even though people can't say that I have bad breath. People so seldom engage in conversation with one another. It's more of a mental thing. The smell. The business about the onions is just an image. A metaphor.

About the man with the windbreaker: He had small hands. Feminine hands. It didn't hurt. Really, it didn't. A little. But not really.

It's also been proven that this type—I'm talking now again about those from the south—perspires more heavily than the northern type. It has to do with the climatic conditions, and it's simple to figure out: Where the sun burns hot, people sweat. No reasonable person would question that.

18

I want to emphasize once again that I have never once sat on a park bench. I swear. By Allah.

He is silent.

I don't believe in God. But you can't compare God and Allah with one another. They are like two different shoes. The one is stretched out and the other too tight. Metaphorically speaking.
German is a beautiful and a good language. Leica. That was my first German word. That's when it began. With the desire. I like to speak German. I have to speak German, although I can't tolerate any more German. German is a fast-acting sleeping pill.
German is an effective language although it doesn't suit me. And because I use German this way, I'm sometimes sorry that everybody uses the familiar with me. There's also the possibility of using the formal with one another. Not because it's more polite. Not at all. It's just nicer sounding. More melodious. To my ears at least. Unfortunately people too seldom enter into con-

versation with one another.

When I get into a conversation, I always say I'm younger than I am. We aren't that precise with the truth. That's proverbial, and there's a little spark of truth in every proverb. I'm twenty-five.

I wanted to say something about Allah. But first I'd like to say again how much highly I regard the German language. That's important to me. With the first money I made I bought myself the best German-Arabic dictionary available. I can show it to you.

He leaves.
He comes back with a thick book.

It cost me 348 roses. When a person arrives in this city, he first buys himself a map, light bulbs, and a package of rat poison. I bought myself the best German-Arabic dictionary. Here!

What I wanted to say about Allah: I eat pork. That's what I wanted to say about Allah.

He is silent.

This is my chair. Here's where I sit. I really like my chair a lot. Of course it's not my chair. According to the laws of ownership. But a person can also love something that doesn't belong to him. I sit in my chair when it seems more sensible than going out. The smell of ammonia. The forty-year-old men. Let me phrase it this way: Even though this chair doesn't belong to me, it's my home.

Here is where I sit and talk into the mirror. I see all of you in the mirror, if I may be so presumptuous. The longer I observe you, the greater my guilt becomes. I mean what I say.

Nabil, who as everyone now knows comes from Port Said, has no right to sit in this chair, even though he is my friend. I would turn him in if anybody came to the door. I would open it and say: Nabil Abbas? Yes, he lives here. Please! The door on the right. He's sleeping. I'll wake him up. I would do that. Not because I'm afraid. With us it's a matter of attitude. Betrayal.

The longer I observe you, the better I think I understand why you have such a deep-rooted hatred for us. It's just a part of a person. Hatred. Deep within, I know. You can't do anything about it. The hatred is so great that it diminishes a person more and more, I know.

Just suppose I would go out, although I know how much the evening hours provoke a person, just suppose I would do it anyway. I'd have it coming to me. I know how much the evening hours provoke a person. So? The broken glass in my face has nothing to do with any of you. It has to do with me. It comes from the inside. Spiritually. I'm totally responsible for that. For evening hours and dark skin.

He uncovers his upper body.

Just suppose the curse word or the iron rod or the knife would strike me here. Right in this spot.

He points to his heart.

Let's say a wound three inches long. We have to start with that. Maybe I would scream, although I wouldn't have any right to scream. Just suppose I would scream anyway, if the curse word or the iron rod or the knife would strike me here. I wouldn't scream because of the pain. And not because of fear. I would scream because all of you were right. I would scream courageously to all of you. That's what I mean by screaming.

Suppose they would drive the broken glass under my skin. I wouldn't scream because of the pain. I'd scream because you are right!

Cut up my penis! Let the tears run from my eyes! Tear open my back! Twist my feet off! When I scream, it's because you are right! I want to raise you up! Stand up already!

PARK-BENCH PEOPLE!!!

He calms down.
He sits down again in the chair.
He closes his shirt.

I take that back. I take it back.
I TAKE IT BACK.

He is silent.

My name is Sad. I sell roses. I don't have
any right to. Because of the license. And I
understand that. Really. Then anybody
could come and sell roses. And God knows!
Roses mix better with a pale skin. Especially red roses. That's been proven
aesthetically.
I sell red roses. Kurt, from whom I'm
allowed to pick up the roses every evening,
knows that I'm an illegal rose peddler. Not
just an illegal rose peddler, he likes to say.
Rightly so. Sometimes a person is in the
mood to joke and then he goes too far.
Insolent, Kurt says. He calls a spade a
spade. I pick up my roses from him. Every
evening at eight. When he closes up his
flower stand. Counted out. He insists on
that. We work well together. I pay for the
roses in advance, and he doesn't ask about
my family name. We don't know anything.
The roses don't know anything either.

24

I don't want to say anything more about Kurt now. He's fair. He can even put up with me, although he suspects that I will cheat him some day.

That earlier stuff that I was screaming about, I take it back. I don't regret it, but I take it back.

He goes away.
He comes back with a bottle of gin.

This damned pride in me. What is it? To do something and not to regret it. Stubborn as a mule. Nabil is that way too. Out there, by the west entrance to the city where he sells his newspapers, which he has no right to do.

I stood behind a chestnut tree. The clouds of exhaust smoke, January. How he races through the line of cars on red and still isn't familiar with the money and can't count it out. He says he needs it: the smell of gas. He says it makes him high. This damned pride!

It occurs to me that in Arabic my name means "the proud one." Sad, the Proud.

He laughs.

Now you caught me good. Sad doesn't
mean "the proud." Now you've caught me.
Actually Sad doesn't really mean anything.
My name was pulled out of thin air. Sad,
that's three letters. My name isn't Albert,
the Shining, or Alexander, who fended off
the enemy troops, or Andreas, the Manly.
In English Sad means sad.
But am I in England, huh?
Now you've caught me.
Cheers.

He drinks quickly.

Lying is a mental thing with us. It's part of
our ancestry.
Very simple.
Now I'd like to say something about my
head: My head is too large. Flat in the
back. The people here are so nice. With
their perfectly proportioned heads. They act
as if they don't notice when somebody's
head is too flat in the back.
And now my lips: Too thick. Blacks and

26

Arabs. The similarities can't just be brushed aside.

And now my skin: It's already gotten lighter. But the pores are still as large as they were. I never wear short-sleeved shirts. Not even in summer. It's not aesthetically pleasing.

And now my hair: As a joke I once dyed my hair blond. With peroxide. The stuff burns your eyes. A stupid thing to do. The ticket controller addressed me formally. Your ticket, please. He said: Your ticket, please. Your ticket, he said. Then he was taken aback, but he didn't let on. The large pores of my skin irritated him. He didn't let on. Your ticket, he said.

I like to ride the subway. I like being in this city. Terribly much so.

I've been circumcised. That's barbaric.

This is my chair. Here's where I sit and wait until it's eight o'clock. Sometimes I wait for twelve hours until it's eight o'clock. I can sit here, for twelve hours. Without moving a finger. Many of us do that. Sit and wait and feel homesick.

Oh, the terrible flapping of the palm

branches, the noise of the bazaar in the background, the unapproachable father, the lost game of backgammon, and the bitter tea. A lot of bitter tea. A lot.

When I speak German, I sometimes still think in Arabic. That's why everything gets confused, and that has to do with the culture and the sun. The confusion. When the sun shines on a person's head for too long, he can't think clearly any longer. The brain doesn't block out the sun. Over the long term or from generation to generation. The sun glared down on my mother's head, on my grandmother's, and on my great grandmother's. Those are facts. And nobody should get excited about the fact that facts can sometimes be very simple. I'm a firm believer in that. And I would advise you to believe it too.

He goes away.

Nabil! It's seven!

He comes back.

I don't speak Arabic with him. In the beginning. Not any longer. He wanted to commit suicide. In the beginning. Four times. With rat poison and laundry detergent. I asked him—in German—why? You have your gasoline high, every night at the west entrance to the city. You have your high. What is it you want? He wants to go home, he says. Home! Home? Where an apple costs five marks?

He swallowed it, the rat poison and the laundry detergent. I run out and telephone. They came immediately. The medic and the policeman. Even though many people are on the verge of death in this city. Valuable people. Park-bench people and forty-year-old men. Those are facts.

The medic puts on a rubber glove and Nabil shits all over his bed and gives his family name. The medic takes off the rubber glove and writes out a bill. The policeman writes down the family name. He had powerful arms.

You're just too sentimental, I shout into Nabil's face. In front of the medic and in front of the policeman. Although I have no right to shout in front of a medic or a policeman.

Now Nabil understands everything. He no longer wants to die, he says. He looks forward to his gasoline high. Where an apple costs five marks, I say. In Port Said, in stinking Egypt. You're not grateful. You don't have any right to your gasoline high, I say. Now he gradually understands. But now it's too late.

Cheers!

He takes a swallow.

I live well. Really. I sell roses. Four marks a piece. To the forty-year-old men who buy themselves forty-year-old women. This is a profession with responsibility. Roses are not just roses. Discretion is the magic word. I can deal with roses. It's a fast-paced profession. I know that these roses will already be wilted in the morning. That has to do with Kurt's flower stand. And I know that the forty-year-old men will have their appetites back again by tomorrow. So a person has to watch his step. Sixty pfennigs

30

for me. The rest in advance. That's a good cut.

Roses have a soul. I always wash my hands. A girl once said to a forty-year-old man—it was at the twelfth stop: Strange. The rose doesn't smell like anything. That has to do with the distance, I replied. This rose, my dear young lady, has a long flight behind it. Of course I didn't say that to her. I bowed and said thank you, although a foreigner really doesn't have the right to say thank you. That riles people up, and they think you're trying to mimic them. Discretion is half the battle. You have to start with the premise that rose peddlers are always a nuisance. Many of us mutter when we don't make the sale. In Arabic. If you mutter in Arabic, you're not a good rose peddler. If you mutter in Arabic, you don't understand the forty-year-old men.

He grabs the bunch of roses.
He walks from table to table.

A rose?

He bows.

Roses?

He bows.

Please. A rose?

He bows.
Etc.

Two days ago. At Ma Pitom. The thirty-eighth stop. Somebody looked me straight in the eye. All of a sudden. Right in the eye. Yellow sweater and hair parted on the left. Yes, hair parted on the left. Right in the eye. And smiled No. Didn't say No. With his hands or with a shake of the head. Right in the eye. Smiled No. Smiled. Right in the eye. To me. Didn't say No or turn away, politely. He smiled No. Right smack in the eye. Right there. In the eye. He looked at me. He smiled No. No. He didn't have to smile. Why did he do that? The man in the sweater. Smile at me. Right in the eye. Right in my black eyes. At Ma Pitom. At the thirty-eighth stop. All of a sudden. Simply smiled. Smiled at me. Sad. The rose peddler. Smiled.

He begins to cry.
He continues speaking.

Damn this sentimentality! He just smiled. He could turn away. He could show surprise at the size of the pores of my skin. My lips could remind him of a black. My head shape of mongoloid children. Damn it! Simply smiled!

He shouts out.

I'm a foreigner! Illegal! Not a Kurd! Haven't been tortured! A foreigner! Not a foreign friend. Don't call me a foreign friend! Because of friendship! Somebody like me doesn't have the stuff for friendship. Betrayal is a state of mind. You all don't know anything about that. I'm different than all of you. Don't think it! Say it! Say it already! One human being is not the same as another! The boat is full! That's

33

enough! We'll never be able to live in peace with one another. And why won't we ever be able to live in peace with one another? BECAUSE I LISTEN TO THE RADIO TOO LOUD!

Have you ever heard a foreigner listening quietly to the radio? He doesn't do it! It won't work! In peace! Because I dirty your display windows with my fingers! Because I shit right next to you in public shit houses! Have you ever seen a public toilet that didn't have shit all over? Then you didn't look very closely! Ask the cleaning women if you don't believe me!

Peace?

Never!

Because your white streets are getting darker and darker! Because I go walking too much! Go take a walk! You'll see me everywhere! The dirty grin and this insolent pride! Where does it come from anyway? It's a shame, one of you notes sadly, that the streets are getting darker all the time!

He goes to the apron of the stage.
With fifty roses in his hands.

34

A person can't even go out on the street anymore without becoming sad or without being afraid. Ask your women. Ask them! And if none of them admits it, she lying. Because she's afraid.
Afraid!
That's the way it is!
Peace! Don't make me laugh! When every day brings new worries! Just listen to your children! Just listen to their German! They don't even learn their own native language any more. Schiller and Goethe. And why? Ask them! Just ask how many foreigners are sitting in their class! Just ask! We have to talk about this.
And haven't you noticed how crude your children have become? Then you're not very good parents is what I say to you! Just listen to the way seven-year-olds speak nowadays! All you hear is asshole, shit, prick, and cunt! That's the way seven-year-olds talk nowadays! Unfortunately it's the truth! But you can't say anything!

He becomes more agitated.

You can't say anything in this country any more. We've come that far already. To think that our children have been corrupted by these prematurely pubescent, so-called foreign friends. That's where we've come to. I'm not a xenophobe. I swear, I'm not. I won't let anybody say that twice to me. But I love my country! I'm worried about my country! And if your country no longer means anything to you, then you are really a sorry case!

Our country doesn't mean anything to the foreigners either. Do you all think they are here because the apples are so cheap? They've got their eye on our jobs and even more so on our social system! That just has to be said flat out! They can never behave properly! Behind our backs they despise us! They are mocking us! Because we're so generous! These people are different!

I'm not saying that they are any less important than we are! I didn't say that! Did I say that they were less important than we are?

But they are different!

They will never cooperate with us! Every one of them carries a knife with him! It has to do with the mentality!
And what do you think! Are they peeling apples with their knives?
So there!
And let me say something else: If things were to go shitty for us, would they then take us in, in Turkey, in Poland, in Rumania, in Egypt, in Iraq, or anywhere else? By the hundreds of thousands? Would they? Things are not going shitty for us, but I ask:
WOULD THEY DO THAT??!!

He begins to scream.

The boat is full!! To hell with hospitality!! A few hundred, a few thousand—okay!! But not an exodus!!
My child is more important to me than hospitality!! He's a happy child!! He has a German name!!
My country is more important to me than anything else in the world!!
I'M NO FASCIST!!!

Nobody better call me one a second time!!
Is a person a fascist just because he worries
about his country?! Is he??!!
I'M NO FASCIST!!!

He loses his self control.

It's a beautiful country!! An absolutely
beautiful country!! They once had a
beautiful country too!! The Turks, the Jugo-
slavs, the Arabs, and everybody else!!
Did I destroy their countries??!! Did I do
that??!!
My child doesn't say cunt and asshole to his
mother!! Not my child!! My child doesn't
carry a knife around with him!!
NOT MY CHILD!!! HE'S A HAPPY
CHILD!!! AND HE'S GOING TO STAY
THAT WAY!!! HE HAS A GERMAN
NAME!!! AND HE'S GOING TO KEEP
IT!!! MY CHILD!!!

He stands motionless
on the apron of the stage.
With fifty roses in his hands.
He stares into an imaginary mirror.

He places the roses in a bucket.
He sits down.
He is silent.
Music which does not seem quite real.
The national anthem.
Softly as if it is not real.

My name is Sad. I'm a piece of shit. I've never contested that. Really, never. I smell myself. I see the pores of my skin. I wash my hands. But I smell myself.

You are all generous. So generous. You have to look at me, every night. You have to wiggle by me. You're so patient. You have to look at my face. So patient. You have to watch me sitting in your beloved subway. You have to see me show my skin in your blossoming parks. See me breathe your precious air. See me eat from your plates. See me stick my fingers into your white bread. Put my lips on your glasses. See me finger your books as I read your language with my black eyes. See me live in your apartments that your park-bench people have willed to your children. Put up with no longer being able to understand the letters on the nameplates of your doors. You are so magnanimous. You are so generous. So patient.

You have to watch me count your money in my hands. Watch how I drink your gin, how I smoke your cigarettes, read your newspapers. Watch me lie in your hospitals. Watch your doctors patch together my decrepit heart. Watch me lie in your sanatoria curing my filthy lungs. Watch me walk along with your shiny brass crutches. Don't be patient any longer. Don't be generous any more. Don't be silent any longer. I carry a knife with me. I'm not peeling apples. Stop trying to understand me. Stop smiling at me. And don't address me so politely. Don't worry about my decrepit heart. Go right ahead and show surprise at my thick lips. Go right ahead and joke about the back of my head. Curse my pride. Ban me from using your door signs. Stop me from sticking my fingers into your white bread. Don't let me stroll around in your blossoming parks. Otherwise what will be left of you? What will remain? Don't be sad. I'm not sad. No, I'm not sad although my name is Sad and I live in a country in which I don't have the right to live. Don't be sad. This is your country. The streets are getting darker and darker. But they are not black yet. The language is still German, and you simply must refuse to listen when people are speaking another language so overbearingly.

Don't listen. Don't be sad. Don't be. Every day brings a little bit of joy. Get up. Go fetch your children from the classrooms where the black eyes are multiplying and where German is disappearing more and more. Schiller and Goethe. Wealthy men with enriching words. Think of Schiller and Goethe. Your children won't say prick and asshole and cunt. They are happy children. Don't be sad.

Don't believe in peace. One day we will overrun you. Protect your children from that. It's time. Close the borders. I know what I'm talking about. But don't be sad.

Shh-shh-shh! Don't be sad! The country still belongs to you. Really! You are citizens of this absolutely beautiful country. You have politicians who are citizens of this absolutely beautiful country. Good politicians. Clear-sighted men. Young men.

Shh-shh-shh! It's time. But it's not too late yet. The clock isn't about to strike midnight. Good politicians. Clear-sighted politicians. Men.

He whispers.

The children! Hey, you've got to get the children out! I'm speaking to you as a friend now. This is important to me. I'm speaking to you as a friend: Do you have a child? A seven-year-old? A happy child? Alexander? Albert? Andreas? Do you want him to say cunt to you some day? Or prick to you? I'm speaking to you as a friend. This is important to me. Is that what you want? Are you going to put up with that?

He talks even more softly.

Shh-shh-shh! Don't say anything. Don't be sad, don't. Get up. Go. Do something about it. Take courage. Give others courage. Harden yourselves like a brick. Like a brick. Pass it on from one hand to the next. Now! Quickly! Go! Your child! Shh-shh-shh!

He is silent for an unbearably long time.

Strange. Before. I mean after I screamed—when I was justified in screaming—I thought for a moment I heard something like music. I heard music. Music. Music from your country. Your music. It sounded as is someone was rattling an iron rod across the gates in the subway. Something like metal clanging. An iron rod probably. Or a knife, or a curse word. More like a curse word. Most like that. Very rhythmical, although I don't have any sense of rhythm. Rhythmical and getting progressively louder. It encircled me. The music. Encircled me. Before. I mean after I screamed. Something like metal. A wrecking bar. More like that. Most like a wrecking bar.
Those were the children of the forty-year-old men.

He walks away.

Nabil! Get up! In three days we'll have electricity again! Go sell your newspapers now!

He comes back.

He's not sleeping. He always wraps a towel around his head. But he still can't sleep. Somebody threw a beer bottle through his window. Harmless. A drunk. For sure. It doesn't matter to me. Since the immigration authorities found out that he's from Port Said, nothing matters to me. A drunk. Really.

He walks away.

Get up, you filthy street swine!! You shit, you!! I want to get the electricity back again in three days!! So go sell your papers!! Get Up!! You stinking Egyptian!! Mother fucker!! You miserable excuse for a human being!!

He is silent.

Didn't you hear me?

Pause.

I said get up!! You foreign swine!! Onion eater!! You who doesn't even know how to shit properly!! You paper-tit-fucker!! You with your stinking mouth!! Get up!! You repulsive rat!!

He comes back.

We often do that. Curse at each other. Just for fun. In the beginning we really didn't mean what we said to each other. It was just sort of a rhetorical thing. We would always burst out laughing. Because it was always just a rhetorical thing. But now we're a bit further along with it. I can say this much—if he gets picked up, I won't miss him. Friendship doesn't have the same meaning for us as it does for you. But the cursing, I'll miss that. Now that we've come a bit further.

I don't want there to be any misunderstanding here. Nabil is the same type of
person that I am. I don't feel superior to
him in any way. The insults are just a kind
of diversion. Both of us really need it
equally as much. The insults. The night
passes quicker. And the eight miles become
shorter and the forty-year-old men smaller.
Just so there's no misunderstanding. Nabil
is my friend. I wouldn't risk my neck for
him. But he's my friend.
I don't want to talk any more about the
relationship between Nabil and me. You'd
get a totally wrong impression.
My name is Sad. My name is Saddam.
Actually my name is Saddam. Saddam is a
first name. Adolf is also a first name, or
Jesus.
I have no right to speak these names in one
breath. I don't regret having said Adolf or
Jesus, I only wanted to say that Saddam is a
first name.
That's why I call myself Sad. In English
Sad means sad. I'm not sad. Am I sad,
huh?
I love the German language. It's a good

language. I once read a sentence. In Arabic. But I know that it was conceived in German. I will speak this sentence now. Not verbatim. I only know it from the Arabic translation. But it was thought up by a man who spoke German. So. Here's the sentence:

That which one cannot speak about, one should remain silent about.

Now I know that the sentence is wrong. The sentence is wrong. At least for me. The man didn't know what he was starting with it. What one can't talk about, one must talk about. That doesn't sound very elegant, but the truth is never elegant.

With a terrible scream.

THE NIGHT!!!!
DIDN'T HE KNOW THAT??!!
THAT THERE IS SUCH A THING AS NIGHT??!!

He starts drinking heavily.

I'm a student. Philosophy has always

fascinated me. And the German language. Now it's your gin, although I have no right to drink away your gin from you.

He walks nervously through the room.

Let me calm myself down and take everything back that I just said. I take it all back. That's the God's-honest truth. That's how I am thinking now. Do you understand why I'm taking everything back?
How will you ever be able to understand me? And how will I get to the point of wanting to understand you?

He reaches into his pocket.

This is my mother. From August 1980. Every mammal has a mother. The mother of a dog is called a bitch. She died from cancer of the uterus. She didn't want to die. But she had to die. When she was still alive, the smell of decay came from her mouth. With mammals that's called wasting away. Although I don't know if female dogs can even get cancer of the uterus. I don't

know. Our dog doctor was helpless. And in the dog clinic too many demands were placed on the dog doctors. Even today there's no treatment for cancer of the uterus in a bitch. In dogland. In dogland there's no such thing as Christmas. That's how degenerate life is there.
This is Her here.

He screams.

Why don't you write me any longer?! FATEMI!!!

Softly.

I want to die.

He is silent.

Really. I live well. I do have my roses. How many people can say they have fifty roses a day in their apartment? Very few people can say that. Really. Few people can say that. That they have fifty roses in their apartment. Every day. Few people can.

Cheers!
Her name isn't Fatemi. I'd never divulge her name. Her name isn't Fatemi. You'll just have to be satisfied with that.
I'm going to go now. I think I can go now.

He extinguishes the candle.
Darkness.
He speaks very submissively.

A rose?

Silence.

Roses for the ladies?

Silence.

Pardon me, roses?

His steps are heard as he walks away.
A door closes.
Silence.
A door opens.

My name is Sad. I'm thirty years old. In

English Sad means sad.

I am sad.

Sometimes a person is in such a mood that he doesn't dare step outside the door to his own house. By that I mean of course the door to the house of my landlord. Just so there's no misunderstanding: The door to the house belongs to the landlord, and on the nameplate is the name B. Winter. The name of the previous renter or of the one before that.

He places the roses in the plastic bucket.
He lights the candles.

B. I've often thought about that. B is a pleasant sounding letter. A feminine letter. Brigitte. Barbara. Beate. It's not important, but maybe a woman with white skin once lived in this room. With white hands.

Oh, the white hands of women!

I meant to go. Really. Even though we're not very careful about the truth. That has to do with our mentality. My God. I really wanted to go out. To get started. The first few feet of the eight miles. The first of the fifty-eight stops. The first of the fifty roses. Tomorrow their heads will be drooping. I wanted to go, I could swear to that, although our kind doesn't have the right to swear. I understand that.

I could stand in front of you and raise my hand and swear: I really intended to go. But...

He sits down.

I want to express my desire to tell you how much I love this country. I have a real need to do so. This beautiful country with its deep-green lakes, its snow-blue mountains, its great culture, and its wonderful thinkers. Of course I only live in this city, in this room and at night, and you could ask me: Have you ever stood at the shore of our deep-green lakes? Have you ever climbed our snow-blue mountains? Have you ever come to appreciate our culture and our wonderful thinkers? You could ask me that. I would stand before you and blush. That is: My face would turn even darker.

I would try to get my head out of the noose

by emphasizing again and again how much I love your country. And the language that is spoken in your country.

Then I would also like to mention once again that I have really never ever sat down on one of these park benches with the cast iron legs.

I'm very particular about this point, I know. Fine, I occasionally use a public toilet. But only when it's absolutely necessary. And as far as public toilets go in general, I'd like to state it this way: It is true that we excrete our feces in an unhygienic way. By we I mean the southern type. That has to do with our misunderstanding of nutrition. But are there not some people among you who occasionally don't eat properly?

I'd like to reformulate this question and say right off that I don't really mean it seriously. The question: Is it always only the foreigner who is shitting next to you?

I said that I don't really mean for the question to be taken seriously!

He is silent.

And now I'd also like to give you a thought to take home with you, so that you no longer have to be afraid whenever you see a few black eyes outside: This is still your country. Don't forget that. Whenever you see a few black eyes, just think: This is my country, and I won't let my country be spoiled by anyone. Certainly not by any foreigner.

That's what you have to think, my friends. Don't misunderstand me! I say friends because of the psychological effectiveness. Don't misunderstand me.

FRIENDS!

For example, you could do the following in the future: Just think every morning about how many foreigners, Turks, Albanians, Greeks, Iranians, Arabs, Poles, Russians, Rumanians—just continue as you wish with the nationalities!—how many foreigners on this day—legally or illegally—will pass through the borders of this country. Think about that as you wake up. Ten? Fifteen? Twenty? A hundred? Three hundred? —Make the number as large as you like!

So.

Then consider—perhaps at your workplace when there's been some irritation—for how many of these immigrants—legally or illegally—am I supposed to actually break my back and pay taxes? For ten? Fifteen? Twenty? A hundred? Three hundred? —Raise the number in accord with how upset you are!

At lunch in your local restaurant—when you determine correctly that the prices have gotten more and more obscene and that they have almost doubled within a year—at lunch you could let your eyes roam around your local restaurant and begin to count: One, two, seven, ten foreigners in my local restaurant. If the number exceeds your level of tolerance, you should definitely change your restaurant!

You should just begin to let the raw numbers speak for themselves and not feelings. You should calculate and just sit down once and seriously think about how all of this is going to proceed.

The rent, for example. Just consider why the rents within the course of a year—we can simply say it—have doubled. Just think about it! And if nothing comes to you, study the door plates in the building where you live. Go down to where the intercom is, stand in front of it and try to read the name-plates. Not so that everybody sees you right away. You could act as if you had forgotten the keys to your apartment. Read the name plates and begin to count: one, two, seven, Antic, Behain, Abbas, ten foreign parties in my building. I'm sure that if you stand in front of the intercom for your building, something will occur to you about the horrendous apartment rents. I'm rather sure of that. Dead sure.

You should let the raw numbers speak for themselves. Not feelings. You should simply count more. And you will quickly determine that counting will become an unbearable habit. Unbearable. You will soon determine that. But you just have to start at that point.

On Sunday afternoon for example. If it's raining and the children are getting on your nerves and have been calling you names like prick and cunt and asshole. Just go down to your street and count the cars. The Seven-series BMWs, the big Mazdas, and the silver-gray Volvos. Just look behind the windshield and begin to count the black eyes.

And if nothing occurs to you as you count the black eyes, just think about the constantly rising interest rates you are paying for credit at the bank.

And just think very soberly, without any to-do: How is it that he can afford himself a Seven-series BMW? How did he get his big Mazda? And how is it that he drives a silver-gray Volvo? And when folks like us try to get a loan, the people at the bank just make long faces.

WELL, IS MY NAME HASSAN??!!

He extinguishes the candle.

I wanted to leave you with that to take home with you. None of you is named Hassan. And when the people at the bank make a long face the next time, just shout into their long face that your name isn't Hassan. You've got to defend yourselves. I wanted you to take that thought home with you.

He suddenly stands motionless.
In the middle of the room.
He appears thunderstruck.
He appears to hear something.
He listens.

I just want to say once again that I'm happy to be allowed to live in this city. That's the truth. Happy, although I don't have any right to be happy in this city. But it's the truth.

He listens.
He is afraid.
He composes himself.
He sits down on a chair.

My name is Sad. I am a piece of shit. I have no right to live. I'm an Arab. Not a Kurd. Arab. Semite.
Sad. A piece of shit. Just lying around. A piece of shit into which others inadvertently step. Sad. The thirty-year-old Iraqi. A piece of shit that others get dirty from.
Shh-shh-shh! Don't be afraid!

He presses his hands against his temples.

Shh-shh-shh! Sad. In English Sad means sad. I'm not sad. Don't be afraid! Sad with the black eyes. Sad, from whom you get dirty, when you look him in the eye. Sad, who buries his dirty fingers into your white bread. Sad, who coughs away your precious air. Don't be afraid.
Don't be afraid, you dirty little Arab! Sad with the thick lips. Sad with the flat back of the head. Sad with the large skin pores. Shh-shh-shh! Don't be afraid.
THEY ARE AFRAID OF YOU!
You become cynical. You dog shit, you! The dirty foreigner is becoming cynical. That's how far it's gotten. This dirtball is becoming cynical. Here illegally and cynical. What a dirtball! Dirty foreigner with his dirty mind. Women's white hands! There you have it! Filthy pig!

He drops his hands from his temples.
He reaches into his pocket.
He speaks despairingly.

This is me. With my bald head. It was when I entered the university. Unfortunately I have my eyes closed. I was always shy about having my picture taken. Philosophy and the German language. Since I first heard this word. Leica. This wonderful word. People really have no idea how much one word can change the world. Leica. The word opened up the world for me. The flight. Basra. The swamps. Teheran. Ankara. Warsaw. Stockholm. And now here. The word has given me strength. I still dream this word today. Leica. Out loud, Nabil says. It's a good word. I haven't deluded myself. No, I really haven't.

That's Her. She is twenty years old. In the photo. She's older now.

In Basra there is an old fountain. The fountain of the travelers. Translated literally. Before a person leaves, he throws a mustard seed into it. Or two mustard seeds. The legend has it that the mustard seed swells up. The legend has it that the mustard seed swells up, even though one will never see its fruit: The legend talks about an underground field. About a blossoming underground field. You have to believe that the mustard seed swells. If you don't believe in the mustard seed, you will never return from the desert. From the desert.

Full of homesickness.

Oh! The night on the roof! As a child I could reach to the stars. With my stinking little paws. To the stars. And when the wind came, the palm branches rustled and flapped.

He imitates the sound of the palm branches flapping.

Oh! And backgammon! Each game a defeat. Akhil was the only one I could always beat. And the sweat of my sisters. And my father in his black caftan. And the thick horn-rimmed glasses. And the red marks on his nose. From the thick horn-rimmed glasses. And the tea! Oh, how thirsty we were! Tea. Always tea! And the sun! Oh! The huge sun!

It's not true. The tale about the mustard seed, I mean. There aren't any mustard seeds in Basra. And there isn't a fountain there either. None of it is true. I lied to you. That's the way I am. Whenever I open my mouth, I have to tell a lie. Even I can't do anything about it. I'm a filthy, lying foreigner.

My name isn't even Sad. My name is Achmed. My name is really Achmed. That's the truth.

He imitates the sound of
the palm branches flapping.

Really. Things are going well for me. I have a roof over my head, and in three days I'll have electricity again. I'll listen to the radio and turn the volume up all the way. Things are really going very well for me. I have my roses. I have my fifty-eight stops. I'll wash my hands every night before I go out. I will say thank you and bow, even though I know that I turn people against me by doing so.

It's time, Achmed. Get going!

He extinguishes the candle.

I would just like to say once more how
happy I am to be permitted to live in this
city. And if the pieces of glass would hit me
now outside, the wrecking bar or the curse
word, I would sink my teeth into the back
of my hand and think out loud:
I WAS FORTUNATE!!
EVERY DAY!!
And I'd like to say something else before I
go. And what I am now going to say, will
have to seem unbelievably overbearing to
you. I am well aware of that. But so what!
Now I'm just being overbearing:
I love you!

There is a noise.
A loud rattling sound.
The rattling of iron bars.
The noise subsides.
A beer bottle is smashed.
The noise is heard again.
First from a distance.

Then closer and closer.
More and more threatening.
An incessant hammering.
The sound of the iron bar
being struck against the subway gates.
He continues to speak.
Unabashed.
The louder the hammering becomes,
the louder he speaks.

At that time. When I arrived by train.
Sweating, tired, and dirty. When I got off
and was standing on the platform and really
saw all of you for the first time. Really saw
you, I mean. Not in magazines and not in
photos. No, really saw you. When I saw
you. Your complexion, the perfect shape of
your heads, the smooth white hands...As
soon as I got out, I loved you. You and
your incomparable language! Your
beautiful, good, incomparable language! I
wanted to say: When I got out, I couldn't
help but love you. I know what it is I'm
saying. And I know that I have no right to
say that to you. Let alone to love you.
And I speak now in the name of many of

us: As we stood on the platform and saw you for the first time, we were entranced. Many of my kind have told me that. It's a feeling that a person can never forget. Standing on the platform and breathing the air and knowing that an apple costs fifty cents. That's a strange feeling!

The noise becomes incessantly louder.
He speaks louder.

Now I know—and many of us know it too—that I should never have been allowed to come! Never! We aren't worthy of this country! This beautiful country! With its deep-green lakes, its snow-blue mountains, its great culture, and its wonderful thinkers! We didn't want you to get dirty because of us! We didn't want that! We didn't know that we are carriers of a disease that infects you, enrages you and makes you violent! We didn't know that! We didn't know that we would never be able to live in peace with one another! We just didn't know! Nobody told us that down where we come from! Nobody told us anything! We only just heard again and again that life in the north is good, and that an apple costs fifty cents! We were deceived too!

The noise becomes unbearable.
A military-like hammering.
He tries to shout over the noise.

My name is Sad!! I'm thirty years-old!! I'm a piece of shit!! I didn't know that!! They never told me that down where I come from!! I can't help it!! You have to believe me when I say that!! And when I go outside now, I won't scream!! None of us will scream!! When the piece of glass is driven down into our skin!! Nobody will scream!! We promise you that!! Just so that you see that we have some class!!
Cut up our penises!! Let the tears run from our eyes!! Tear open our backs!! Twist off our feet!! Nobody will scream!! Because we know what we have done to all of you!!
Get up!! Go out and strike down each and every one of us!! You park-bench people!! Get up!! You forty-year-old men!! Get up!! You children of the forty-year-old men!!

Get up!!
This is your country!! These are your cities!! Your towns!! Your deep-green lakes!! Your snow-blue mountains!! This is your culture!!
SAD DESTROYS EVERYTHING!!
SAD IS EVERYWHERE!!
SAD IS GETTING BIGGER AND BIG-GER!!
SAD IS MULTIPLYING MORE AND MORE!!
GET UP!!

The noise reaches the threshold of pain.
The national anthem.
As if a gigantic chorus were singing.
As if a gigantic orchestra were playing.
The light comes on.
Someone continues grumbling.
The words are no longer understandable.

MY NAME IS SAD!! I'M THIRTY YEARS OLD!! IN ENGLISH SAD MEANS SAD!!! I'M NOT SAD...

Darkness.

This play was written in Fall 1991. It is dedicated to Salih, the Iraqi, who taught me about Vienna and taught me that fictional stories are the best stories.

Afterword

Robert Schneider created a sensation on the German literary scene in fall 1992 with the publication of his novel *Schlafes Bruder* (*Brother of Sleep*). Several months later, in January 1993, his play *Dreck* (*Dirt*) premiered at the Thalia Theater in Hamburg and cast the author into a leading role in contemporary German theater as well. The enormous success of these two works and the subsequent interest they sparked have established Schneider as a prominent figure in the literary and artistic debates of the German-speaking world.

Despite the widespread attention he has received, Schneider's success has been neither immediate nor rapid. His decision to embark on a literary career can be traced back to 1985. In an interview from 1992, Schneider acknowledged that he had been writing unsuccessfully for years. Interestingly, after he completed the manuscript of his bestselling novel in 1990, the work was rejected by more than twenty publishers before finally being accepted by Reclam Publishing in Leipzig—to whom Schneider had never personally offered the work! In some cases publishers had considered the appeal of the sensitive artist novel about the impassioned composer Johannes Elias Adler too limited, partly because of its rural Austrian setting in Vorarlberg, and in others failed even to review the manuscript before rejecting it. In light of the publishing industry's disinterest in the novel, it is ironic that Schneider's recent meteoric rise to fame has been accompanied by the support of the German-speaking world's most feared and harshest literary critic. After having read the novel during the fall book season of 1992, Marcel Reich-Ranicki labeled the author one of the few promising talents on the German literary scene.

Within little over a year of its publication, the author had signed contracts for translations of the novel into seventeen languages. To date *Brother of Sleep* has been published in approximately thirty languages, including English, and the German edition alone has sold copies well into six figures.

70

A film version of the novel directed by Joseph Vilsmaier is scheduled for immediate release, and an opera composed by Herbert Willi will premiere in Zurich.

The reception of Schneider's play *Dirt* has been equally remarkable. During its first year there were roughly forty original-language stagings, making it currently the most performed play in the German-speaking world. Its minimal theatrical and technical requirements and provocative contemporary theme have aided the adaptability of the one-man play to a variety of venues. A ballet version was performed in Kaiserslautern in fall 1993.

Robert Schneider was born illegitimately on June 16, 1961, and raised with three other adopted siblings by foster parents in the town of Meschach in Austria's Vorarlberg region. Despite the limited cultural resources of the rural surroundings of his youth (there was scarcely a book in his home), the author's parents supported his budding inclinations towards music and literature. After completing the Gymnasium in 1981, Schneider commenced his studies of composition, theater, and art history in Vienna but in 1985 made the decision to interrupt them in order to begin his career as a writer. After six years in Vienna he returned to his native mountain village where he currently resides. Since the late 1980s, Schneider has been the recipient of numerous awards, most notably a grant from the Abraham Woursell Foundation in New York in 1990 and the more recent Salzburg "Prix Eliette" in 1994, of which he was the first recipient.

Riding on the crest of his present success, Schneider's previous work has attracted attention as well. In an early play from 1988, *Traum und Trauer des jungen H.* ("The Dreams and Sorrows of the Young H."), Schneider strives not to explain the phenomenon of Hitler but rather to display the pitiably impoverished nature of his character. The play, which draws on the chorales of Bach's *St. Matthew Passion* to introduce each scene, is comprised of eleven monologues from what Schneider describes as the totally undistinguished, mediocre life of the young Hitler. For Schneider, Hitler was neither Nietzschean *Übermensch* nor predestined demagogue elevated by fate. Schneider has also written another play dealing with Hitler, entitled *Hitlermein— Eine Liebesrede* ("My dearest Hitler— Words of Love"), which premiered on the dictator's birthday in 1989.

Schneider maintains that he writes solely for the enjoyment of writing and that no latent Oedipus complex or horrific childhood experiences are lurking in his subconscious for him to uncover. He has consciously not developed a concrete writing style but rather considers the theme of each of his works the determiner of its appropriate language and voice. In musical terms, the author becomes the instrument playing compositions with their own uniquely specific content and form. As a result, Schneider considers his works essentially distinct from one another, much as musical compositions of different periods in differing styles. His most famous play and novel illustrate this situation quite clearly.

Beyond the obvious difference in the genres of play and novel and in their respective urban versus rural settings, the writing styles of Schneider's two successes contrast sharply. The language of *Dirt*, a monologue by an Arab from Basra, is simple, straight-forward, and conversational. Far removed from the typically broken slang of foreigners, it is well-groomed and idiomatic—despite its occasional vulgarities. The language is unusual perhaps only in the fact that it stems from the mouth of a foreigner who has had only limited opportunity to master the tongue of his adopted home. The impact on native speakers that this linguistically accurate invasion of their world has is rendered all the more powerful when one considers the foreign source. Sad, the societal outcast, communicates clearly and coherently in the contemporary idiom of his host country.

Brother of Sleep, on the other hand, blends an artistically refined language deriving from the cantata texts by Bach with dialect expressions from Vorarlberg. The work's title originates from a Bach text "Kömm, o Tod, du Schlafes Bruder" ("Come, oh Death, you brother of sleep"),

74

and reflects the main character's artistic, musical nature in counterpoint to the novel's rural mountain setting.

In light of the author's musical proclivities, it is not totally surprising to learn that he resides more comfortably within the framework of music than that of literature and appraises the influence of musical models on him higher than the literary ones. Music inspires Schneider and its experience evokes words and images, whereas literature often has the effect of developing writer's block in him. In a recent interview Schneider reestablished this view of himself as a musician who finds himself less content in a purely literary environment. Schneider's use of crescendo in his writing is an example of his adherence to principles of musical composition.

For his Hitler plays as well as for *Dirt*, Schneider has delved thematically into society's repressed consciousness and the undigested dregs mired in its maw. However, a significant difference among these works is that while Schneider, as a second-generation postwar writer, shares only an historical relationship to Hitler and National Socialism, his experience with foreign workers and the discrimination they endure is first-hand. The source of Schneider's fictional character is his friend Salih, an actual rose peddler from Iraq with whom the author lived in Vienna. Salih's humor and irony mixed with sadness and homesickness parallel Sad's experience, and thus Schneider's fictional text assumes its own penetrating reality.

At the core of *Dirt* lies the intensifying spiritual and psychological distress experienced by its character. Psychological pressures weigh down Sad and over time lead him to believe in his own inferiority. The rose peddler's vain attempt to merely disappear behind the unforgiving societal backdrop is thwarted by the brutal conditions of the everyday environment. It becomes painfully clear how little room the status quo affords to anything foreign. In the end, Sad, the illegal alien without rights and without legal claim to asylum, both acquiesces and revolts as his screams hidden by the noise of the subway symbolize.

Society's perceived need to preserve
its identity through adhering to aggressive
fictions is poignantly exposed in Sad's
monologue. Beneath society's apparent
order and its xenophobic aesthetic lie its
own twisted deformity. The attention drawn
to Sad's physical distinctiveness—his dark
skin, odd-shaped head, black hair, and large
skin pores—merely serves to reveal the
Western world's true soul.

Is Sad's monologue a justified attack
on the status quo or merely a personal
existential outpouring in the form of interior
monologue? In effect, Sad's consciousness
is divided and split between his loyalties and
desires. He is both himself and the other.
Yet in attempting both to preserve his Arab
ethnicity and to assimilate himself into his
German-speaking surroundings, Sad begins
to lose his identity and humanity. Not even
his near total command of the native language can ameliorate the deep-rooted senti-
ments he confronts.

Sad's experience as outsider is, of
course, not unfamiliar to the author himself.
His early childhood as an adopted son estab-

lishes a common thread among all his works. Schneider states: "I always felt like an only child, and my great happiness was to be left alone. That way I could do my things alone and sketch out my world." It is his own search for self-identity that filter into the powerful monologue of *Dirt* much as it does into the artistic nature of Johannes in *Brother of Sleep*. In *Dirt* as in the Hitler plays, the author unleashes his unabashedly engaged, provocative socio-critical ire. For Schneider, the role of the writer and artist is to grapple with political problems. This is the artist's moral obligation, even though its truth is never elegant. Schneider has repeatedly relished his role as *provocateur*.

The play's reception in the English-speaking world should prove no less powerful and provocative than it has been in the German-speaking one. Despite the scenario of foreign workers in an otherwise homogeneous Western European society, the author's theme strikes at the heart of prejudice and discrimination in its multitude of forms and manifestations. Schneider's outlook remains staunch and undefeated as he fulfills his role in ensuring that this world not be destroyed before our very eyes.

Paul F. Dvorak
Virginia Commonwealth University